THE BIG WORLD
ACCORDING TO
LITTLE HUNTERMAN

CROISSANT EDITION

LEGENDARYMEDIA
PUBLISHING

FUN AND SERIOUSLY COOL DOGGY WISDOM FOR
DOG LOVERS

THE BIG WORLD
ACCORDING TO
LITTLE HUNTERMAN

HOW TO FIND FRIENDS, DEFY BATH MONSTERS,
AVOID CROISSANT SHORTAGES, CRUSH DOGGIE
WORRIES, AND TOTALLY MANAGE YOUR HUMANS
(WITHOUT MISSING A NAP)

THE FANTASTICALLY ILLUSTRATED
CROISSANT EDITION

BY

HUNTER LASSAL

LEGENDARYMEDIA
PUBLISHING

First published in 2019 by LegendaryMedia

eISBN: 978-3-86469-076-1
Hardcover ISBN: 978-3-86469-077-8
Paperback ISBN: 978-3-86469-078-5
CROISSANT EDITION
Version 4.0a

A catalogue record for this publication is available from the
German National Library (DNB)

LegendaryMedia e.K.
Windmuehlstrasse 4 • D-60329 Frankfurt am Main, Germany
www.legendarymedia.de

LEGENDARYMEDIA
PUBLISHING

Little Hunterman is a work of fiction.
Please be sensible with your dog's diet, care, training, and exercise.
Never consult Flynn. Always consult real experts!

TO MY FRIENDS AND COMRADES ALL OVER THIS EARTH-BALL.

ESPECIALLY TO THOSE WHO LOVE ME THE MOSTEST.

CONTENTS

PART 3

TOTAL INTRODUCTION-THINGY

Life can get tough at times. And, just like bright angry-sky flashes, bad stuff can strike out of seemingly nowhere and be really loud and scary.

When it gets hard to stay on top of stuff and properly care for our home-places and humans, loving doggie advice can help big time and totally save the day.

In this book my rubber duck, Flynn, and I will show you how to find cool new friends, steer clear of becoming bath monster fodder, avoid being fed boring icky stuff, deal with crippling doggie worries, and totally manage your humans.

All very useful doggie advice, right?

It pays to have loving and trustworthy friends you can rely on when danger looms and the ground gets shaky.

But first thingies first:

THAT'S ME AND ME, YAYYYYY!

Surprise: There are two of me!
Totally coolest, right?

Seriously, though, the world might be full
of mind-boggling mysteries, but how I, a
totally for real Parson Russell Terrier,
ended up becoming a fearless cartoon doggie,
is definitely one of the mostest mind-
boggliesting mysteries of them all.

(Right up there with why we have to put up
with evil bath monsters.)

No one ever found out what fantastically magical forces made my human come up with my cartoon doggie-self (but it must have been a truly earth-ball shattering event).

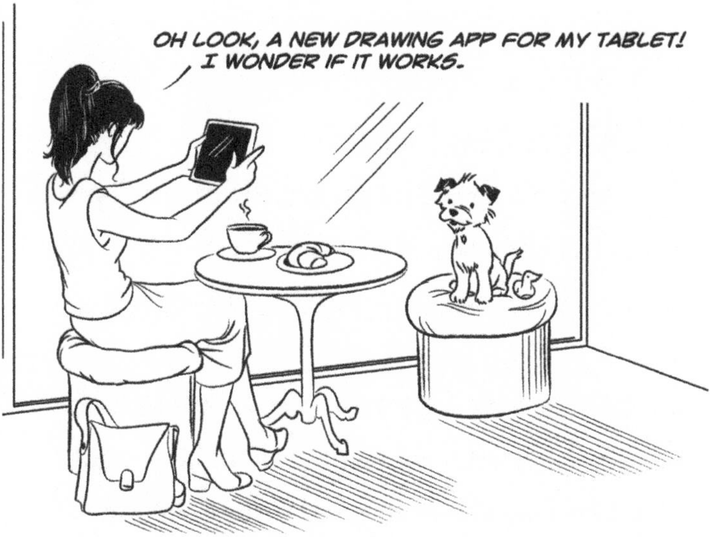
OH LOOK, A NEW DRAWING APP FOR MY TABLET!
I WONDER IF IT WORKS.

Come to think of it, no one ever figured out why I became obsessed with croissants, either.

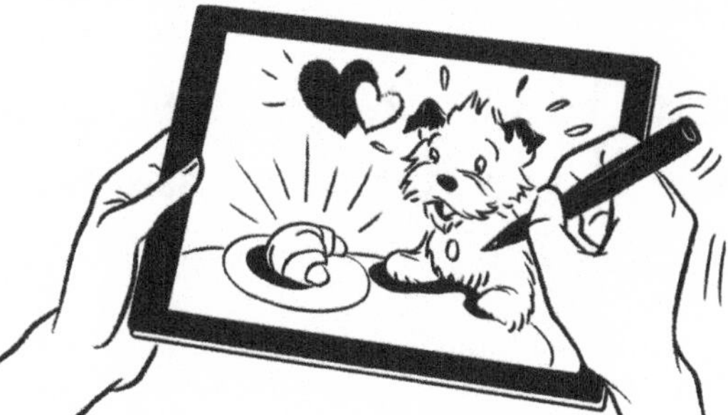

Then again, if my human had only drawn me a wee bit bigger — just so I could've reached the yummy croissants on my own...

(And then humans wonder why we doggies have to beg.)

But that's life, I guess:
All the bits and pieces are never really well thought through ahead of time.
Life is a fill-in-as-you-go kinda thingy.

So that's why I try to do just that: to fill my life with as much fantastical stuff as I can manage — like with long walkies in the rain, which are THE bestest doggie-nose treat EVER! Even though Flynn would never join me on those. He fears rain like crazy.

And, to be fair, it is totally my fault he's so scared of water. It's a sad but true little story.

See, while I was still a puppy, barely months old, I had to make my first big dog decision:

To comfortably stay with my doggie family in a totally safe, predictable, and orderly home-place...

SOMEWHERE IN THERE, THERE WAS A BOUNCY BALL...

... MAYBE.

... or to follow my newfound humans to a fate unknown and possibly full of mighty challenges and life-threatening doggie-dangers.

Obviously, this was a total no-brainer for a fantastically fearless Parson Russell Terrier like me.

And so I went into the wild to conquer the world.

I even got my very own little bed in my very own little basket. Plenty of undisputed room just for me. I liked it a lot.

My basket contained a fantastically soft cushion and an extra orange blanket. Then I would add my mostest important toys of the moment, the ones I thought I wouldn't be able to live without. I'm sure you know what I mean. Everyone has things they think they cannot live without. Even humans, right?

And some nights, when I simply couldn't seem to decide on what I needed, I'd totally try to stuff ALL of my toys into my basket. Then it would get a tiny wee bit crowded.

Then, as the weeks passed, I started to notice the terrible dangers that lived in this new world — like sudden gushes of wind coming from kinda nowhere, weird shadows moving all by themselves in front of open windows, and other totally worrisome stuff.

From that moment on, it felt much safer to close the front gate of my little basket house for the night.

At least at first, it did feel safer.

But because I was not used to being alone, I'd get terribly upset when I'd wake up all by myself in my basket in the middle of the night. So my human let me sleep next to her.

This way all it took was a quick sniff to check that my human was with me and that both of us were safe. That's the magic of a fantastically powerful doggie-nose for you. (It also helped to sleep on my human's hand just to make sure.)

The new arrangements made me feel much less anxious.

Then again, it did not take me long to find more stuff to worry about.
From my newly elevated sleeping-place I could

see right through the apartment window onto the big, unknown outside world.

And my doggie logic told me that WHATEVER was out there would now totally see me, too!!!

Thankfully, we found a satisfactory way to deal with this new nighttime threat.

Big bonus: I'm a winter doggie — so these were my very first flowers EVER! And they were orange, too, my mostest favorite color. Coolest, right?

With my nighttime worries solved, I could

finally fret over my daytime problems. That's because my new human did this crazy work-thingy, see? And even though she usually worked from home, she could not keep playing with me non-stop like she had done in the first weeks.

I had to find new things to do...

... and new friends to do them with. That's how I met Flynn.

Fortunately, it turns out that I'm a total expert in making friends.

Too bad that I had already chewed off his tail, though, turning Flynn into the first ever rubber-duckie afraid of sinking. It made him a wee bit grumpy.

See what I mean?

Flynn's proper name is Admiral Flynn van Kwiitsch, from the Mighty Everlasting Rubber Duck Fleet. He comes from the China-lands which sit on the other side of the Earth-ball from where we live today.

When it's day over there, it's night right here and the other way around.

Weird, right?

Even after crossing the big Pacific-Ocean waters to our side of the Earth-ball, Flynn never got used to the switched around day-and-night rhythm.

That's why Flynn is always awake during our nights and mostly asleep during our days. We try to make the bestest out of it by taking turns watching each other's backs.

DAYTIME WATCH SETUP.

zzzzzZZZZZZ

At night, while I sleep, Flynn reads books or secretly borrows my human's cell-phone thingy to wander the interweb-places.

NIGHTTIME WATCH SETUP.

zzzzzZZZZZZZ

He gets to read the mostest amazing stories.
And then he tells me everything during our
morning walkies (until he falls asleep, that is).

It totally works for us.

And that's also when we prepare our
fanstastical Monday Cartoon Wees.
(You can sign up to get these via wee-mail
on my website, if you want.)

In our Monday Cartoon Wees we talk
about our adventures and other totally
important doggie stuff. And then, once
we have enough cartoon material that
fits together, it all might end up in a new
Little Hunterman book.

Just like the stuff in this book is from our
first ever batch of cartoon-wees.

Coolest, right?
If you go on reading, we'll totally show you.

"What do you mean by
this was YOUR breakfast croissant???"

THE BEGINNINGS
The Story's Big Nose

PART 1
High Priority Doggie Stuff
(And Other Thingies to Watch Out For)

I. LOVE

PUFF!

Let's start by catching the biggest rat and tackling the totally mostest important stuff for any doggie on this Earth-ball: LOVE. Love is EEEEEEVERYTHING!!!!!!!!!!!!!!!!!!

I keep trying to explain this to my best friend Flynn — but he just shrugs. Then again, he's a rubber duck. Rubber ducks have a different outlook on life. Maybe it's the plastic, you know? It must be the plastic...

For a doggie, though, no matter if it's family love, or comrade love, or duck love, or whatever love, there just can never EVER be enough — even more so if love comes with a good ear-scratchie or a cool rat chase.

In fact, love is so fantastically important that it is total madness to expect it to pop up by awesome magic or crazy coincidence...
... and to stick around for no apparent reason.

You need to always make sure that enough fresh love keeps flowing your way.
FORCEFULLY, if need be!

As soon as your humans start losing themselves in their daily work...

... immediate and urgent action is called for.
The earlier you jump on the problem, the better.

Humans tend to get much too distracted by their boring work-stuff to think about love overly much. Once they have found love in their lives, they seem to take it for granted and stop paying any attention. Yeah... Crazy, I know.

Like when they assume that a nice belly-rub in the morning will cover our belly-rub needs for the entire day...!

They forget that without constant love-signals, ten doggie-minutes (even FIVE doggie-minutes) will turn into a bleak eternity of worrisome doggie love-doubts!

4

The trick, therefore, is to surprise your humans in a way to leave them neither time nor room to overthink stuff. This way they cannot come up with lame excuses (like that they need to finish work before having time to show their love).

The more stressed out your humans seem to be, the more important your reaction becomes.

In this case you need to make the love-feedback absolutely fool-proof and impossible to miss!

And then you need to keep repeating these steps every 2 minutes or so.

Remember, humans are forgetful:
REPETITION IS EVERYTHING HERE!

2. LONELINESS & FRIENDSHIPS

One reason why love is important is because it's so terrible to feel lonely.

Doggies are not meant to be lonely. Not ever, EVER! Neither, by the way, are cartoon doggies. We are not made for solitude, or empty little beds, or blank sheets of paper. We need a lot of company and attention.

Yet, at the very beginning, when my Lassal-human came up with my cartoon, there was NO ONE around to talk with!!!!!!! I had no friends. No one cared. Life was dark and hard.

Sure, I had my little rubber duck. I had Flynn from the get-go — but I still felt like there was all this emptiness around me where there should have been a million-trillion friends!

If not more.

Don't listen to Flynn. He does not know how it feels... He likes being alone. It must be that plastic thing.

And I'm afraid that my need for many friends disappoints him.
He seems to be happy enough with just me around and wonders why I don't feel the same.

And why don't I feel the same?
I cannot say for sure.

Maybe it is because Flynn mostly sleeps all day.
Maybe it is because he is made out of smelly
yellow plastic. Maybe it is because he is always
just reading books when he's not asleep.

I just know that I need a lot of friends and
loved ones around me to be a happy little non-
lonely doggie.

However, making friends can be incredibly hard
when you are the new dog in town, when you
don't know a single duck, and when you have no
clue about the local rules of the place.

It's all rather unfair, right?

Just when you feel the mostest desperate, things seem the hardest. I never understood this part of life.

Flynn likes to say that life is totally NOT trying to be logical nor fair.

Maybe he is right.

Flynn has been around for a while.
He knows these things.

FIRST RECOGNITION
OF AN ACTUAL FRIEND

SECONDARY EFFECTS

Strangely, it does get MUCH easier to find friends the more friends you already have.

It must be some sort of gravitational-thingy.

The more we care about the same things, the easier making friends seems to become.

You know, I love to share my stuff with whoever needs it — even if they don't really notice that I exist. It makes me happy.

Caring for each other helps all of us!

Sharing can be totally easy, like when my humans give me icky sick-food instead of the good stuff. I'll gladly share THAT with others.

And sometimes sharing is VERY hard, like when all I have to share is a yummy croissant.

Once you know what to look for, though, you can find friends in the oddest places and under the strangest circumstances.

Take my Friend Mona, for example.

I met Friend Mona in a big art-house place while my Lassal-human was checking on flying-construction thingies for Flynn.

Friend Mona lives in a country where everyone eats croissants all the time. She knows of some fantastical croissant-recipes including several yummy doggie friendly ways to prepare them.

And suddenly, it turns out that Friend Mona is afraid of mice — she keeps seeing them in her huge living-room at night when all the humans leave. So I quickly promised to visit her occasionally to keep her place mice-free. She was so happy that she introduced me to everyone she likes.

See? It's all easy to make friends as long as you care for croissants and mice.

So, now you know! ☺

3. THE WORRIES OF A LITTLE HUNTERMAN
I. Worry. A. Whole. Lot.

I started worrying as soon as I arrived on this Earth-ball and have not found a reason to stop yet. There is a lot more to worry about than I feared.

And, if you think about it, this is worrisome all by itself.

What if the moon won't rise tomorrow? Or if two of them show up? Or if the moon starts rising backwards? Or if it shows up all green and blue?? Or if someone takes a big bite out of it???

Quite the worries, right?

And these are just moon-related — don't even get me started on all the rest!

After a lot of agonizing and many sleepless nights, I decided that the only way I'd stay sane was to face my worries one after the other.

And thereafter I tackled the first one that crossed my path: the worrisome Mondays.

LITTLE HUNTERMAN'S "IGNORING MONDAYS" MOVEMENT

EVERY TIME I IGNORE A MONDAY LONG ENOUGH IT MAGICALLY GOES AWAY ALL BY ITSELF.

That was a major breakthrough!

I learned that there are several kinds of worries and the trick is to go at them separately.

I found that single worries are so much easier to manage and wrestle down than trying to takle more of them all at once.

The Monday-Worry, for example, can be totally solved by simply looking the other way!!!

(Much like the Mirror-Worry!)

The good thing about a Monday is that, if you only ignore it long enough, it'll go away all by itself. (Unfortunately, mirrors are much more stubborn...)

This tactic is important to know because Mondays have the naughty habit of returning every week or so, which is very annoying, indeed.

But if you stick to reusing the "Ignoring Mondays" approach, you'll be on the safe side.

And, granted, some worries do not pass at all when you try to ignore them, but get worse instead!!! That is why I said that not all worries are created equal, which is why we have different worry-categories in the first place.

So, if things get really ugly there is always Plan B: HIDE!

That, by the way, is exactly what my real self is doing here.

(And, yeah, it's totally cool to hide with friends.)

Only experience will tell how long you'll have to stay under the chest of drawers.

It would therefore be clever to stash some food down there just in case.

4. FLYNN

a.k.a. Admiral Flynn van Kwiitsch

Flynn is a tiny rubber duck with a big head full of the mostest strange information.

He fills his head by reading like crazy.

When others sleep, he reads. When others eat, he reads. When others play with friends, he STILL reads!

Flynn reads all the time.

Mostly, he'll read sweet cowboy romances. But when he runs out of cowboy romances, he'll read all kind of other stuff.

He is mightily intelligent and full of advice.

And he stinks.

LiTTLe HUNTeRMaN

A FRIEND IS SOMEONE WHO KNOWS YOUR
WEAKNESSES AND LOVES YOU
JUST THE SAME
- VERY WISE DOGGIE -

Why he stinks, you ask?

Well, unlike his fellow rubber ducks he is not
very fond of water. And THAT would be
putting it mildly!

Basically, he'd rather melt than touch the wet stuff.

Since I chewed off his tail several years ago he panics at the sheer thought of having to have a bath.

That's because now that he has a hole in his little plastic body, poor Flynn is totally afraid of sinking, getting lost forever, and being forgotten by everyone.

It does not matter how often I tell him that this cannot possibly happen in a bathtub.

Yeah, I know, chewing his tail off was a terrible thing to do. But I was just a puppy, and I was bored, and I had no clue that Flynn was even alive!

As you can see in the next photo...

... Flynn now got a coolest prosthetic tail from our Friend Nancy in the America-Lands.

He totally loves to wear his new tail-tip when he dresses up.
(It always makes me smile.)

But he still won't get close to water.

I think what Flynn really is afraid of is getting lost in the deep, dark oceans never to resurface.

Plastic does not die, right?

So, imagine ending up on the bottom of an ocean in total darkness for the better part of eternity?

That's a really scary thought!

And there is no way you can read books down there to pass the time... It would therefore be a total Flynn-HELL!

And that is why I don't tease him about his smelliness.

At the same time, Flynn fears to be recycled into a water bottle or something of the kind — a worry he seems to share with all my other plastic toys.

And before you laugh...
... it DID happen to his great-grand-uncle, who ended up in the recycling bin.
(That's how Flynn inherited his Admiral-title, by the way — it's a rubber duck family thingy.)

We are still trying to find Flynn's great-grand-uncle in his current reincarnation and have been calling out to every plastic bottle we pass on our daily walkies.

HAVE WE MET?

So far, though, no luck.

Nowadays, I carry Flynn around with me to make good for my naughty past deeds.

And one day, I hope to find a way to fulfill his biggest dream: to FLY!

LiTTLe HUNTeRMaN

FLYNN, DAYDREAMING

ZZzzzZZzzz...

5. MOUNTAIN GOAT REINCARNATIONS

The longer you live, the more croissants you can eat!

Flynn is all about living forever. I guess that is normal behavior for a rubber duck. I, on the other paw side, concentrate on what I think is much, much cooler: Reincarnations!

LITTLE HUNTERMAN

SO WHAT?!
NEVER SEEN A *MOUNTAIN GOAT REINCARNATION* BEFORE?

Of course, after each new reincarnation you do get a bit out of practice on some past-life skills. But what do we have our humans for if not for these tiny lapses of reincarnation-judgement?!

Let's not forget that my past life as a mountain goat serves me well while fulfilling my self-assigned daily shredding duties.

All is well in Little-Hunterman-Land whenever
I get a package to shred.
    Or two...
        Or three...

Shredding is simply sooooo totally mega-cool,
that there can never be enough of it!
I, therefore, absolutely LOVE my mail-human
who keeps bringing me new boxes full of
shredding-surprises.

And come to think of it, there might be other
reincarnation-gems hidden in my past...

LITTLE HUNTERMAN
ROCK STAR REINCARNATION

6. WEE-MAIL

If you ever wondered how my comrades and I exchange information: We leave wee-mail messages all over the place!

Wee-mails have many advantages: They are easy to leave on any surface, quick to overwrite, and they take only a sniff to read.

It also makes you look very cool when you stand on 3 legs without wobbling.

That is quite a feat, actually (the 3 legs thingy).

That being said, wee-mail communication does get its fair amount of spam — mostly from cheap dating and walkie services — but you learn to recognize and ignore this kind of stuff.

LITTLE HUNTERMAN

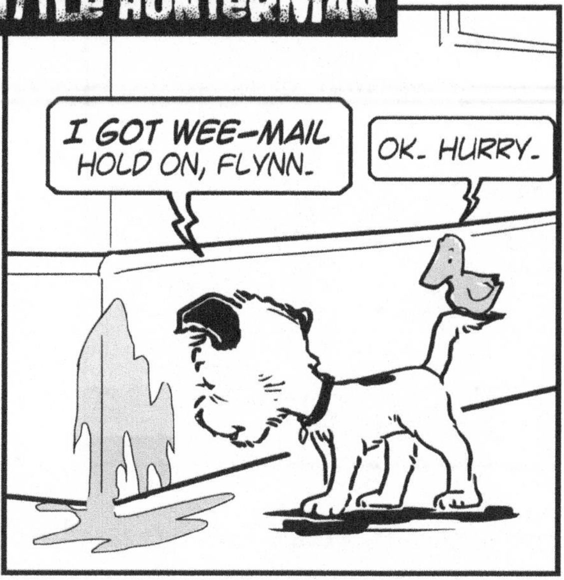
I GOT WEE-MAIL HOLD ON, FLYNN.
OK. HURRY.

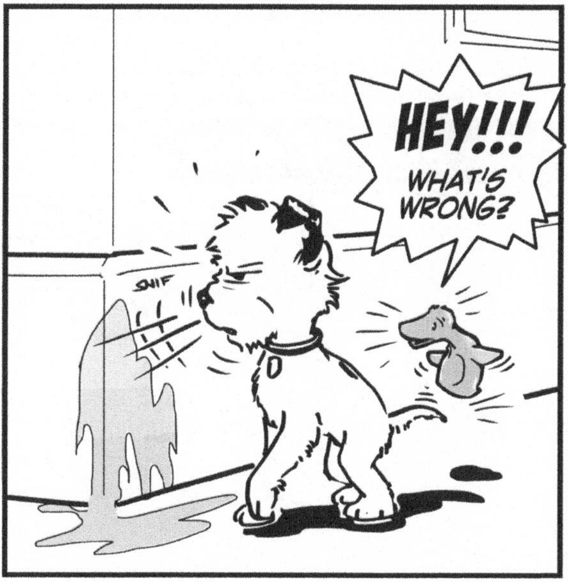
SNIF
HEY!!! WHAT'S WRONG?

Recently, though, because of increased human impatience, it's becoming more and more difficult to finish our wee-sentences.

But there will also always be doggies with too much time on their paws, who go on and on and on... and never seem to find an ending.

Unfortunately, this long-windedness is hard to keep up with and often leads to drinking-problems.

By the way, I write wee-mail not only for comrades, I also write wee-mail for my human friends.

It's a special non-smelly sort of wee-mail that you can read on monitor-thingies.

While it takes more effort to write this sort of mail, you can send cool extra stuff along with it, like extra doggie cartoons!

Kinda neat, really, to keep in contact with friends and comrades who live on the other side of the Earth-ball and to be able to send them stuff!!!

If you leave me your wee-mail, I'll write you one as well.

7. RELATIVITY DEFINITELY DEPENDS

Have you ever noticed how life can be wonderfully easy and totally complicated at the same time?

It makes my little head spin.

And I hear so many humans saying that we should not over-complicate stuff, right? But that is just sideways-thinking because, in real life, small things can make ALL the difference!!!

Or take size, for example.

I'm so little, you know? And humans keep telling me that it does not matter because size is supposed to be "relative".

However, I'm very much afraid that this is only an excuse to make me feel better.
Because, to be completely honest with you, this relativity-thingy does not make much sense at all.

ME!

There are many serious situations when size is of the upmost greatest importance, like when you are trying to relax and sleep on your Lassal-human's lap.

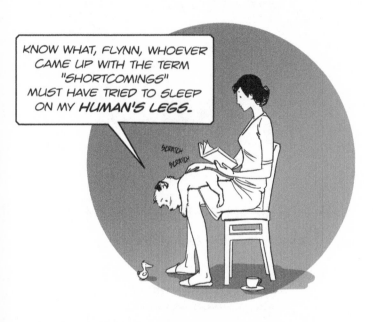

I love her very much, but there is absolutely nothing "relative" about hanging over the abyss!

Just saying.

8. MASTERING THE ART OF THE BALL

Mastering the art of the ball requires a whole lot of concentration and practice.

And concentrated practice requires a whole lot of intensive ball-naps.

A well-rested doggie will always find surprising ball-mastering techniques to keep his humans on the edge of their seats.

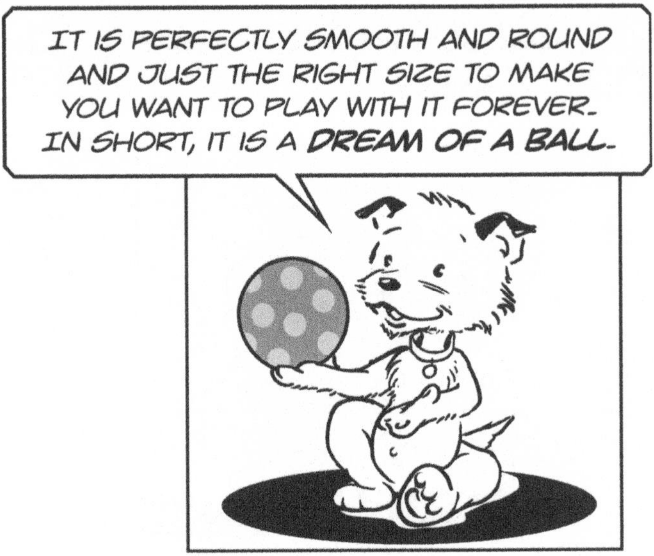
IT IS PERFECTLY SMOOTH AND ROUND AND JUST THE RIGHT SIZE TO MAKE YOU WANT TO PLAY WITH IT FOREVER. IN SHORT, IT IS A **DREAM OF A BALL**.

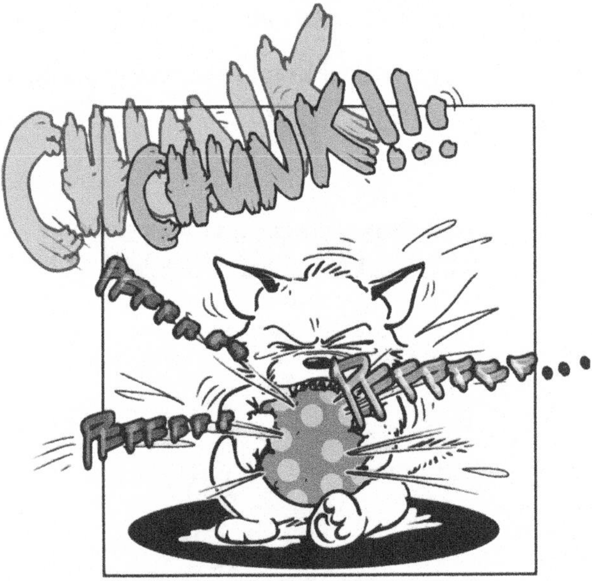
CHUNK!!!

Admittedly, there are more ways to put a ball
into good use.
Like using it to bait your humans!

But more on this fantastically practical lesson
later in the book. ☺

9. WALKIES 1.0

A.k.a. the "sooo last century" style!

We live in a city full of stacked human houses with a huge river snaking right through the middle of it. And our human-house-place is not only stacked real high up in the sky, it is also right at the riverside.
That's pretty cool for walkies, short or long.

Unless, of course, the weather is bad, and the sun is out.

In general, though, our walkie-riverside is a peaceful place.

But like any kind of "peace," ours is constantly under threat!

So we make a point in going out together to guard our territory from mean river rats, crazy geese, and unruly pigeons.

PART 2
The Rules of the Game

10. GOOD DAYS, BAD DAYS, AND THOSE STRANGE DARK THINGIES INBETWEEN

We all have them, right?

I'm talking about those awful bad days, when you don't know which way things will turn out no matter how much you worry, and fret, and wail, and toss, and turn.

LiTTLe HUNTeRMaN

THERE ARE DAYS,
WHEN MY GREATEST
ACCOMPLISHMENT
IS JUST TO KEEP
MY HEAD ABOVE
MY PAWS.

There are good days, too, and lukewarm normal days. But normal days are much less interesting. And they leave a much smaller imprint.

LiTTLe HUNTeRMaN

GOOD DAYS. NORMAL DAYS. BAD DAYS.

Basically, my dark side reflects how I feel.

49

Some people become really good at hiding their dark sides. I'm NOT one of them.

My dark side even has a name: she calls herself Baghaval. And she's a cat. On normal days, at least. Not quite sure who the others are.

Unfortunately, like any cat, Baghaval does not seem to have a single worry in the world, all the time in the universe, and an infinite source of patience as a bonus — a mostest unsettling combination.

She also does not talk much.

Yet, you can easily persuade her to play a round of chess. (Which I'm terrible at, as I prefer to chew my pieces to nudging them around on some weird board-thingy.)

Flynn is very suspicious of Baghaval; maybe because she is a cat. Then again, we all have our dark sides. Flynn is no exception.

See, I told you so!

* * *

11. THE TOTALLY IMPORTANT DIFFERENCES BETWEEN FOOD, FOOD, FOOD, AND FOOD

I'm a terrible eater. At least that is what my humans say. I, however, beg to differ.

The thing about food is that there are totally different kinds of it: there is <u>food</u>, foOD, FOOD, and then there is fOOd. At any given time in the universe thingy, one or more of them are just plain wrong!

Seriously! Food can totally misbehave.

It's just a matter of waiting long enough for it to happen.

Let me show you, okay?

Below is my bowl. Full of strange food-stuff. Now let's wait...

Waiting...

Waiting some more...

SEE?!?
I told you so!
It always happens.
Always! ALWAYS!!! AAAALWAYS!!!!!

Sometimes, though, the food is actually kinda okay but the serving schedule is a mess.

And sometimes I get food that does look like something else altogether.

A totally valid question, right? Unfortunately, my humans have proven to be quite difficult to train in the food department.

Often, I must go to extremes to achieve any positive results at all.

And yet, none of my efforts can guarantee acceptable results.

That is why I have to come up with my own innovative solutions.

Which brings us to a whole DIFFERENT and much TASTIER subject: CROISSANTS!

12. CROISSANTS

Finally!

First, croissants are not food. Croissants are croissants, and yummy, and therefore always deserve to be mentioned on their very own account.

They also deserve to be eaten more often. Unfortunately, no one listens to me.

I would do almost anything for a croissant.

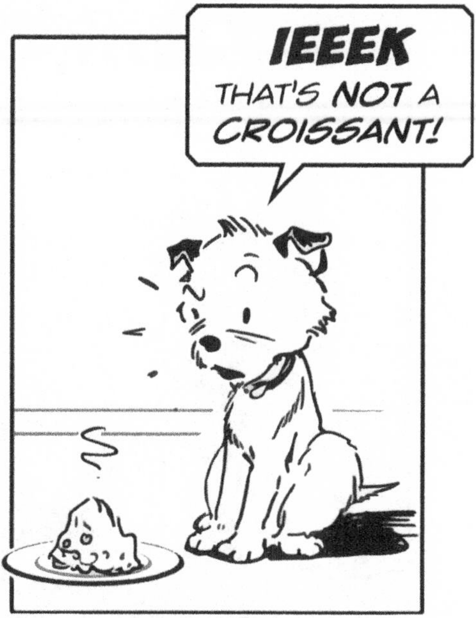
IEEEK
THAT'S NOT A CROISSANT!

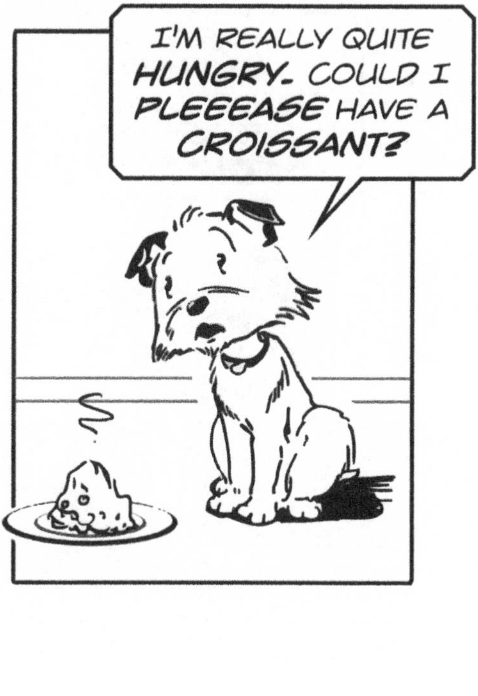
I'M REALLY QUITE HUNGRY. COULD I PLEEEASE HAVE A CROISSANT?

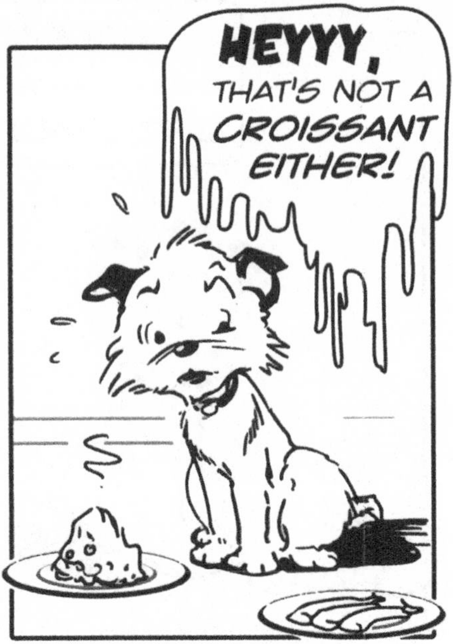
HEYYY, THAT'S NOT A CROISSANT EITHER!

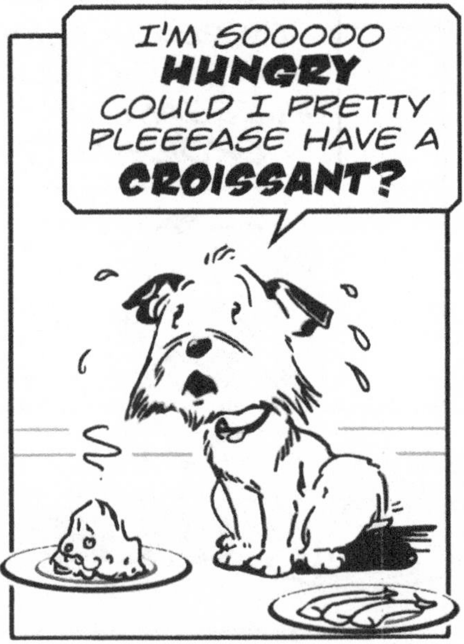
I'M SOOOOO HUNGRY COULD I PRETTY PLEEEASE HAVE A CROISSANT?

So, I started to grow them behind the house.

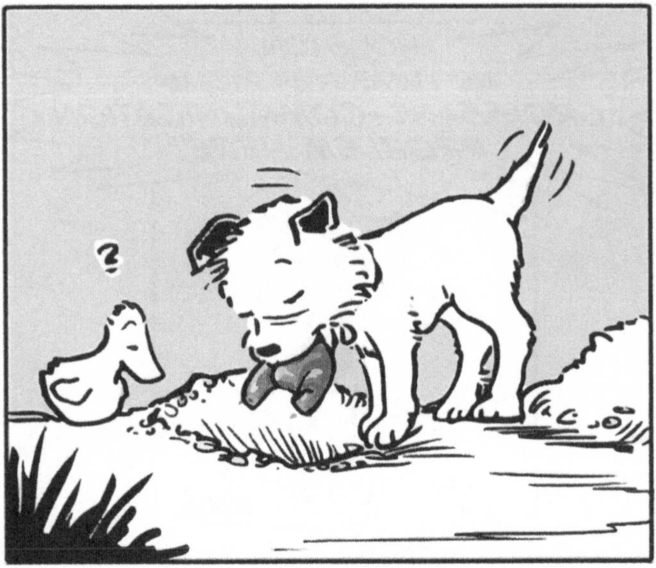
?

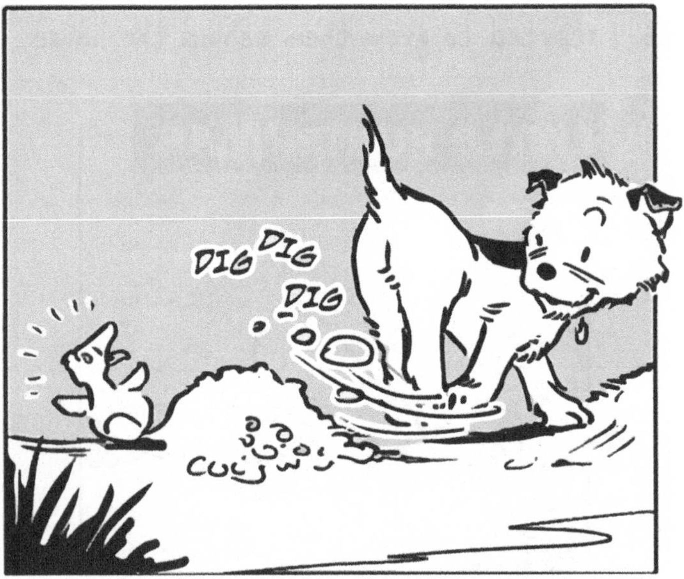
DIG DIG
DIG

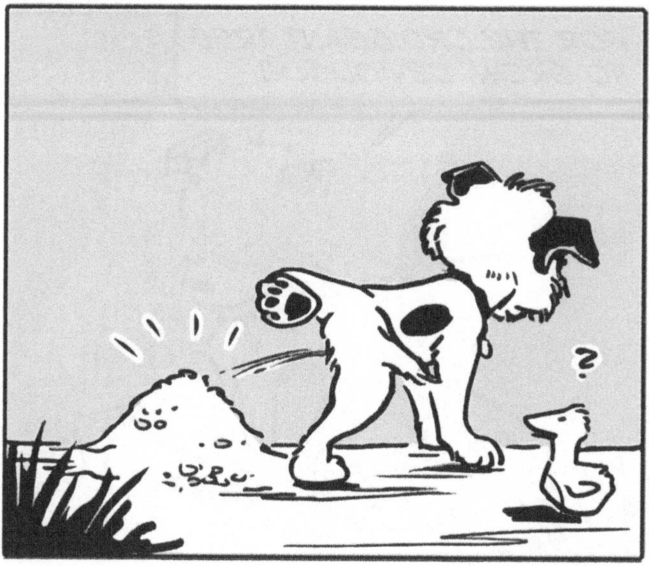
?

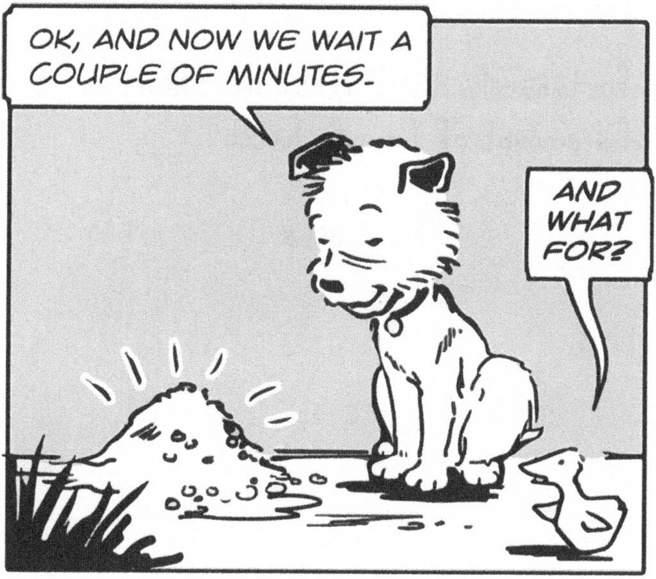
OK, AND NOW WE WAIT A COUPLE OF MINUTES.
AND WHAT FOR?

Unfortunately, these trees are taking an awful amount of time to hatch.

* * *

13. BATH MONSTERS

Now, let's keep our voices down and face the ultimate threat:

BATH MONSTERS!!!
(Hush! Or they'll hear us!!!)

It is in the nature of the mostest dangerous monsters of the whole wide universe-thingy to stay out of plain sight.

I guess that's what makes them so scary: you know that they are out there, somewhere, but you can never be quite sure where EXACTLY...
... and WHEN they'll sneak up on you for that horrible final swipe.

Bath monsters are no exception.

You know that they are in the water, hiding under the foamy white soapy fluff, but when you finally spot them it is most likely too late for a clean (and dry) escape...

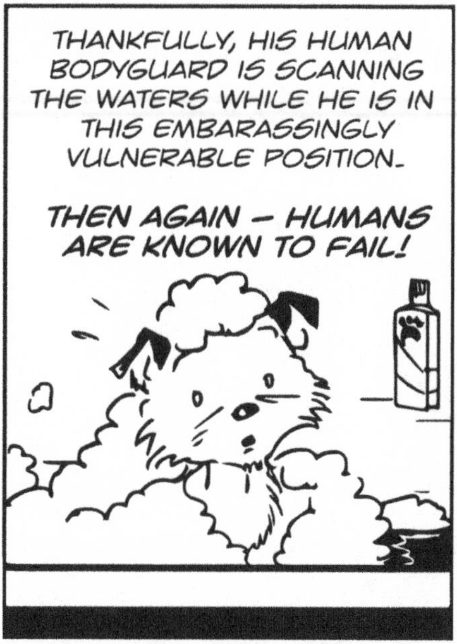
THANKFULLY, HIS HUMAN BODYGUARD IS SCANNING THE WATERS WHILE HE IS IN THIS EMBARASSINGLY VULNERABLE POSITION.
THEN AGAIN – HUMANS ARE KNOWN TO FAIL!

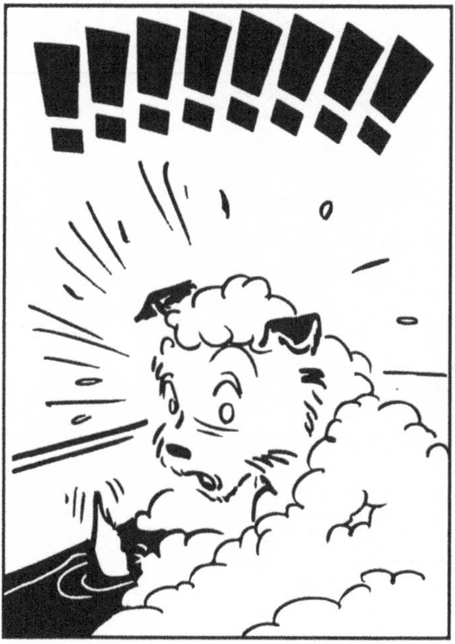
!!!!!!!!

And Flynn obviously does not know what he is talking about.

See, there is little me stuck in the danger zone... Again!
No idea why my humans keep doing this to me.

HELP?!

14. ROUTINES

Routines are totally important to keep us doggies organized and productive.
It is astonishing how much you can achieve by merely investing a few minutes into the same daily tasks.

How many sticks you can carry home and pile behind the entrance door,...

... how many croissants you can eat on top of your supper,...

... how many rats you can chase along the river bank,...

... how many humans you can get to squeal when said rats run over their feet,...

... how many pieces of dog-food you can hide in the bed under your human's pillow (for bad times),...

... or, how many tunnels to China-land you can dig in between nap times.

Little things, done regularly, can add up quite quickly. Same goes for routines in general. That's why there is always a danger of doggie-overwhelm.

Never underestimate daily routines!

15. ABOUT BEING EXTREMELY HELPFUL

One way to assure that your humans will always want to keep you close is by becoming indispensable.

Like with most useful thingies in life, there is a secret trick to this as well!

The trick is to never wait until they ask you to do stuff. Instead, you need to think ahead and solve the problems before they pop up.

It is actually not all that difficult.

One example:
We doggies have amazing talents, like our intuitive complex-geometry-problem-solving thingy: We always find the middle of stuff.

We know where to bite into a sausage (to split it in half) and how to balance a large stick between our teeth so we can take it home

The key, then, is to use this talent to solve the mostest pressing problems of human-kind.

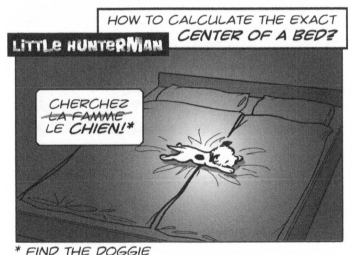

* FIND THE DOGGIE

See? Easy!

And just like that, your humans won't know how to survive without you. Coolest, right?

16. HAVING THE WEES

When I was smaller, people kept staring at me while I was doing my wees. My wee-logic differed from my comrades' — something I was completely ignorant of at the time.

I had assumed that the mostest sensible thing to do is to lean against stuff while lifting one leg. Just to steady myself, right? Even more so when I had to go out in the middle of the night and my human was swaying just as much as I was.

She leaned against the tree.
I leaned against the tree.
And all was well.
Or so I thought.

Then I would notice everyone staring. And by this I really mean...

...EVERYONE!

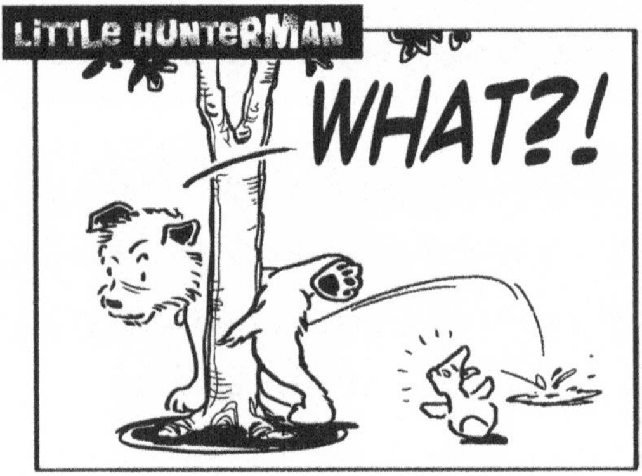
LITTLE HUNTERMAN
WHAT?!

It was very disturbing.

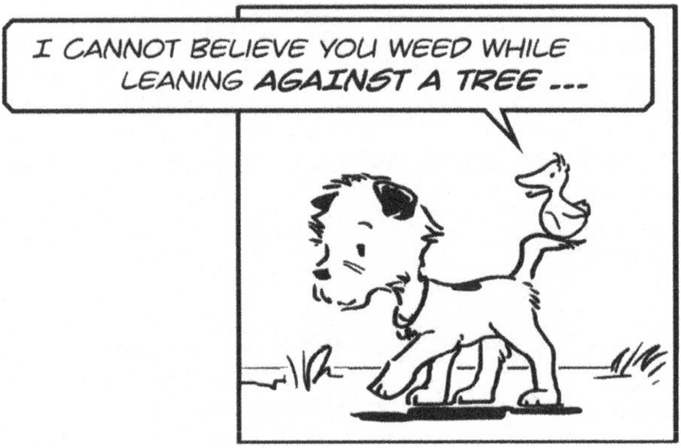
I CANNOT BELIEVE YOU WEED WHILE LEANING AGAINST A TREE ...

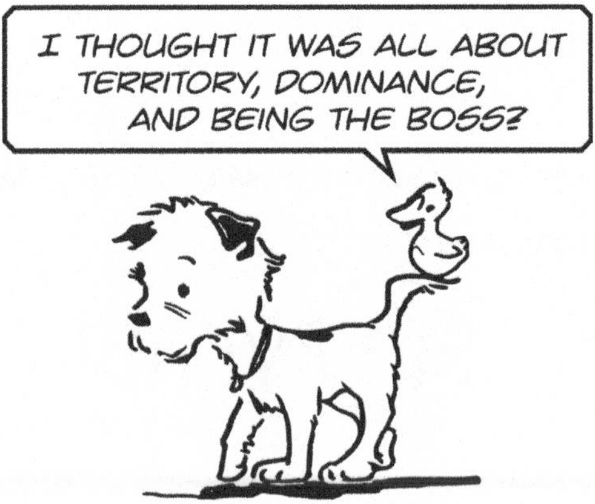
I THOUGHT IT WAS ALL ABOUT TERRITORY, DOMINANCE, AND BEING THE BOSS?

They just don't get it. We doggies can be very practical thinkers.

At least when you are a puppy.

Later, I learned that part of growing up was to prioritize logic. So, while safety and ease-of-wee were a higher priority when I was young, looking cool and totally in control is all that matters when you are playing the grown-up doggie game.

Unfortunately, trying to look cool and totally in control leads to a whole lot of extra challenges.

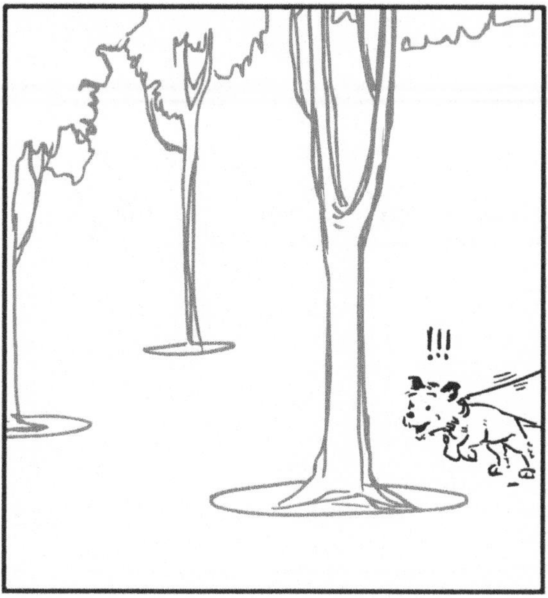
!!!

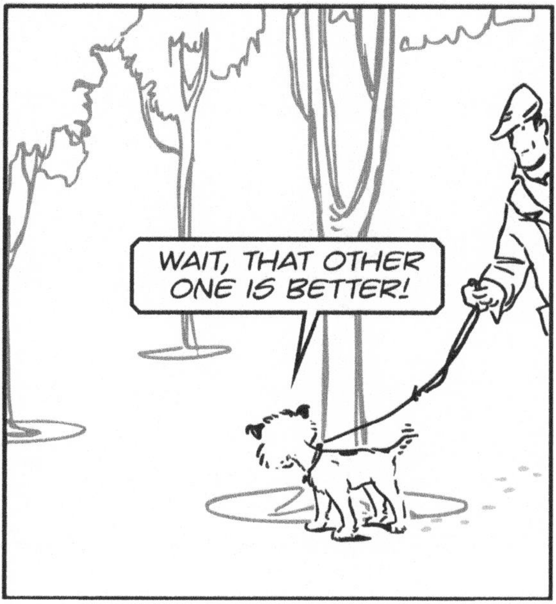
WAIT, THAT OTHER ONE IS BETTER!

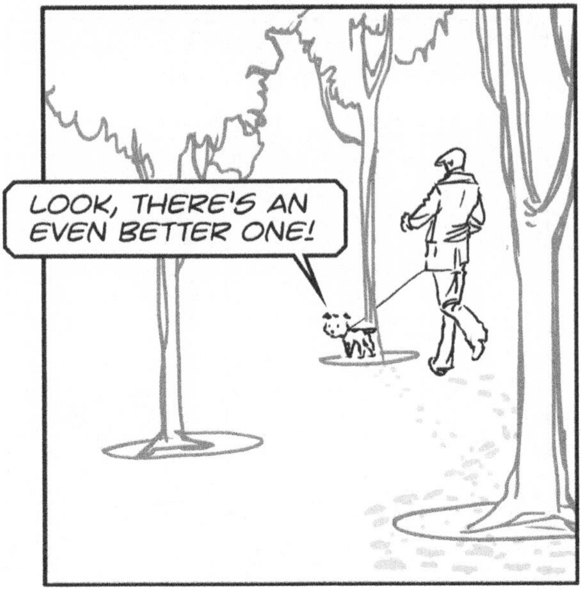
LOOK, THERE'S AN EVEN BETTER ONE!

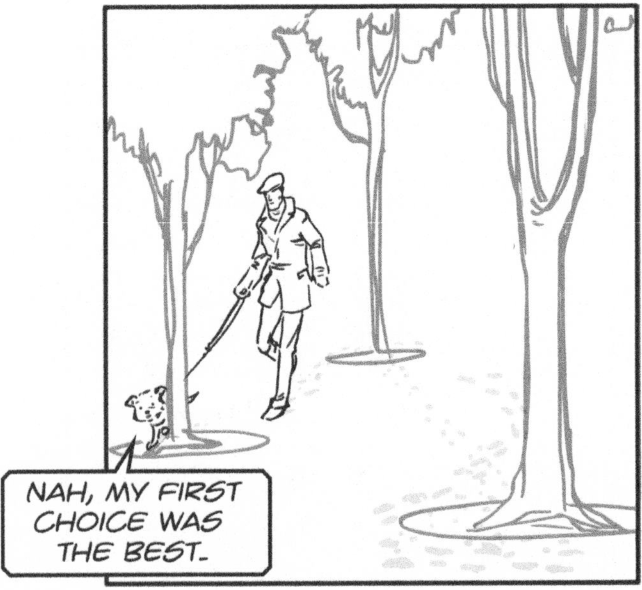
NAH, MY FIRST CHOICE WAS THE BEST.

After all, if APPEARANCE is all that counts, then there could always be a better looking opportunity around the next tree.

Maybe. Right?

17. NIGHTTIME BUSINESS

Have you ever had really vivid dreams?

Like when you can actually smell cold mountain dream-rivers on a hot summer dream-day, taste its fresh dream-waters on your dry dream-tongue, feel how delicious and soothing it is when it runs down your dry dream-throat... right into your little dream-bladder?

Sometimes, my vivid dreams mislead me. But it is always an honest mistake. I swear.

And sometimes, my humans even thank me for it.

Because, let's be honest, the bestest time of the day is the night. So, we should always make the mostest of it and share it with the ones we love.

18. REASONS TO KEEP A HUMAN

(or two)

I know that some of my comrades wonder about the usefulness of keeping one or more humans.

Yes, they can be difficult to handle and they can cause random acts of MAJOR embarrassment...

LITTLE HUNTERMAN

... NOT BEING WOLVES ANY-MORE, SOME OF US NEED HELP FROM OUR HUMANS DURING WINTER TO KEEP WARM.

But they usually mean well. So don't be too harsh on them.

Never forget that humans provide some very serious advantages that totally speak in their favor.

Take the human bodyguard service for example. It can be rather useful...

... as long as you stay in control of the whole situation, that is.

Or take the free poo service...

Flynn keeps saying that this is the service that really shows who's the boss in the human-doggie relationship.

Unfortunately, this service is often quite faulty. A lot of things can go wrong during its course of action.

And while the service was made up by humans and is fully carried out by humans, a faulty poo service often results in humans being mad at us doggies!

As if we had anything to do with it?!

Still, mostly, the poo service keeps our paws clean and avoids spreading the wrong territorial messages all over our homes and resting places.

And that is a good thing, right?

At least it keeps the peace among doggies and reduces human house-keeping tensions.

Which brings us straight to the next point.

Excessive human-shelter maintenance is a must for my humans and a total mystery to me.

Why would you care about removing doggie hair and muddy paw-prints from the floors only to cover them with carpets and sheep-skins instead?

Makes absolutely no sense. Especially if it cuts down on our walkie-time.

On the other paw side, speed-sliding on freshly cleaned wet floors can be lots of fun.

And having a whole lot of fun can leave you plenty hungry!

Which leads us to the seriously cool catering service that humans can provide.

(Especially when they try to bribe a bad eater like me.)

94

Needless to say, everything food-related could be sooooo easy if they only gave me a plate full of croissants in the morning.

- I would be happy.
- They would be happy.
- And it would be less work.

Just saying.

So, in case you've wondered why I'm totally sure that my humans are workaholics...
... now you know.
They simply LOVE unnecessary work!

Then again, everything has two sides, right? And having humans who enjoy extra rounds of work is a seriously cool thing when you plan on keeping your own paws free.

For me, for example, as a hunting doggie, it is totally important to be ready for action and free to pounce at any given moment.
After all, you never know when the next naughty RAT might cross your path!!!

NO STICK ... --- IS EVER TOO BIG --- --- FOR A TERRIER!

BUT SOMETIMES IT IS CLEVERER TO USE (HU)MANUAL LABOR.

That is why you should never feel bad about letting your humans carry your stuff. (Apart from the fact that they seem to enjoy it.)

* * *

I have already explained the amazing benefits of a good croissant-diet, right?

But croissant-logic is just one more of those things that my humans need a little help with.

HUNGRY...
HUNGRY...
!!!

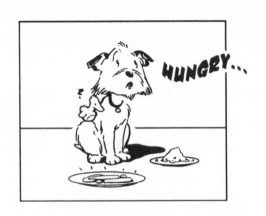

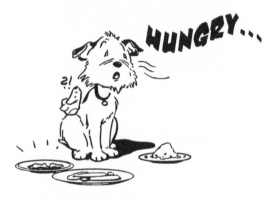

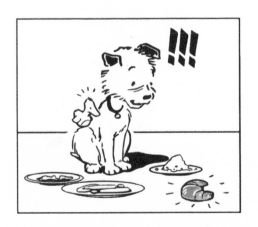

TRUST ME ON THIS, FLYNN, TRAINING HUMANS IS ALL ABOUT *PATIENCE.*

At home, it is all about whose patience keeps the upper paw: theirs or mine.

The upper paw wins big time.

And another seriously cool thing about humans is that they like to leave the upper paw to their doggies.

See? There are a million reasons to keep a human and to love them dearly.

(And I have not even talked about smelly socks! Smelly socks are a total bonus.)

19. DOGGIE-HUMAN COMMUNICATION

In the last chapter, I hinted at some of the most common communication problems between us doggies and our humans.

At the end of the day, communication problems are quite unnecessary. After all, we doggies are famous for our elaborate tail talk.

Humans who can read our tails are pretty much in the know.

Check out my Christmas-present-unpacking tail-communication, for example:

LET'S SEE WHAT I GOT FOR CHRISTMAS!

A NAIL CLIPPER!!!!!

CLEAN SOCKS?!

*WHAT DOES IT MEAN:
"THIS ONE IS FOR THE CAT"?!?!?!*

SOAP!?!

YEAH, A BALL, A BALL!!!!!!

Some humans go waaaaaay beyond that and develop a rather eerie sixth sense which definitely has its downsides.

LITTLE HUNTERMAN

HUNTERMAN, HAVE YOU BEEN PLAYING IN THE LAUNDRY BASKET AGAIN?!

SOMETIMES I COULD SWEAR THAT MY HUMAN HAS
SUPER-GUESSING-POWERS!

On the other paw side, the same sixth sense can also be rather useful.

I guess it is just one of these things in life that we doggies have to live with and make the bestest out of.

* * *

20. LIVING WITH HUMANS

(What it takes)

I've already mentioned a lot of aspects that result from living with humans.

Let me add a few more.

It is important to realize the enormous responsibility we doggies accept when it comes to keeping our humans happy and healthy.

That includes making sure that they stay mentally active and alert. Which you can manage easily by adding little fun surprises to their otherwise boring days.

THERE IS JUST ONE WAY TO IMPROVE A GOOD CRIME MOVIE NIGHT

As the doggie in charge you have to constantly come up with fun and engaging games.

DIG DIG
DIG
SCRATCH
SCRATCH SCRATCH
SCRATCH
SCRATCH
SCRATCH
DIG DIG
DIG

It's a never ending labor of total doggie love.

And it is a bit more work if you have to take care of TWO humans!

Mostly, it all comes down to keeping your humans engaged and reward them with quick payoffs of reassuring nose-nudges and happy tail-wags.

See?

There is a lot of back and forth included, but it usually pays off quite well between the rooms.

Humans find it very important to believe that they control stuff.

Even uncontrollable stuff.

They try it over and over. Rinse & repeat.

It keeps them busy and fills their days.

I guess they like it this way.

The whole matter only becomes problematic when it leads to unnecessary doggie-work.

Then it will be up to you, the aware doggie, to get everyone out of the loop as quickly as possible.

See why it is important to stay on top of the action?
But with the right mindset, living with humans can be quite fantastically fun!!!

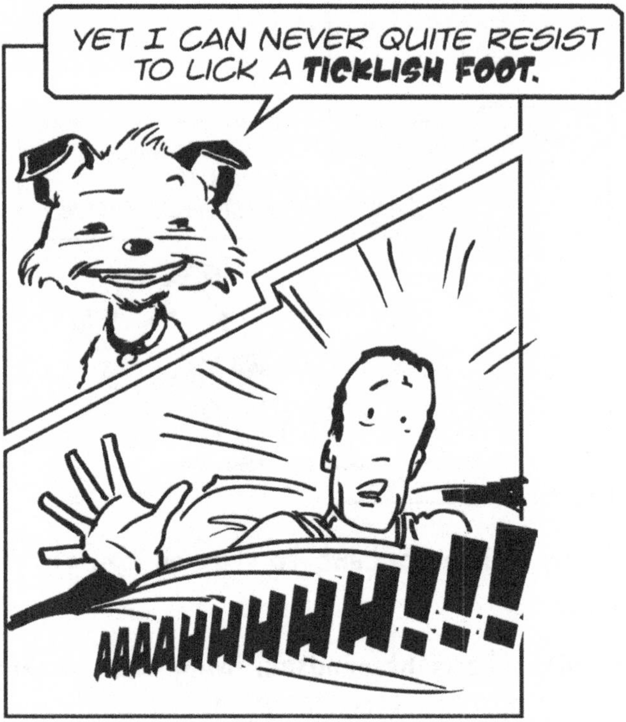
YET I CAN NEVER QUITE RESIST TO LICK A TICKLISH FOOT.
AAAAHHHHHH!!!!

* * *

21. RATS AND OTHER PRIORITIES

With everything and everyone constantly wooing for our attention, it is totally important for a little Parson Russell doggie to keep his priorities straight.

Then again, this is mostly not much of a challenge.

And humans catch on after a while...

22. NAPS, BLACKOUT SLEEP SESSIONS, AND LAZY SUNDAYS

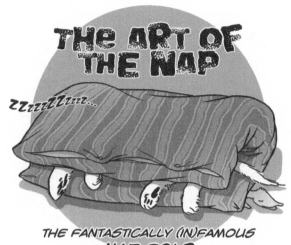

THE ART OF THE NAP

zzzzzzzzzzz...

THE FANTASTICALLY (IN)FAMOUS
NAP FOLD

Speaking of priorities (see last chapter), there are a lot of ways to go about prioritizing stuff.

Take naps, for example.

All of our naps might look the same for an unsuspecting human.

But, obviously, they are not.

If you take a closer look, you will find that there are many telling distinctions.

Standard naps,...

... Lazy Sunday cushion relaxations,...

... deep blackout sleeping sessions,...

... cushion-hugging whack-naps,...

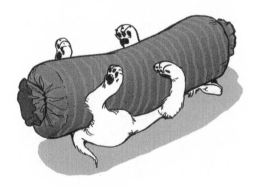

... floorboard readings,...

... dirty-laundry-smell-paradise-naps,...

... Crazy-Monday-pretending-it's-not-real-offline-modes,...

... snooze doggie yoga,...

... minimalist nap-naps,...

... Lazy-hot-Sunday-belly-breeze sleep relief,...

... non-universe-denting naps,...

© LASSAL

... just-hanging-in-there sleeping sessions,...

... and sooo many more.

Did you see how TOTALLY different they are?
Coolest, right?

Soooooo...
... the bestest way to learn the benefits of the different nap-types is to sleep right through the whole list.

Easy, right?!

THE ART OF THE NAP © LASSAL

ZZzzzZZzzz...

RRRRRRRR...

HOT DOG WITH
A SIDE OF DUCK.

It's also the fairest way to go about it, I
think. After all, you would not want your
floorboards to feel left out, right?

(Or your humans' bed to become depressed.)

Take a nap and be happy!

And then take another one and be happier still!

Yay!

* * *

PART 3
Fixing Fixable Stuff

23. BEFORE & AFTER ME!

Before my humans found me, they must have lived incredibly sad and troubled lives. I seriously do not know how they got through the days without a loving doggie at their sides.

Take their clothing choices, for example. What my Lassal-human used to wear was woefully inappropriate for an animal with no feathers nor fur.

LITTLE HUNTERMAN

BEFORE & AFTER HUNTERMAN
EVIDENCE #07350221

BEFORe

AFTER

That was one of the first things I fixed.

Also, when they went about their days, they were mostly rushed, inattentive, and with no one to keep them company, nor to hold them accountable.

I fixed this one pretty quickly as well.

I guess that the mostest important difference is that my humans now have someone in their lives who not only has their bestest interest in mind but who also takes the necessary steps to get to the desired results!

And besides:

LiTTLe HUNTeRMAN

NOTHING COULD POSSIBLY BEAT
SEEING YOUR BELOVED DOGGIE
FIRST THING IN THE MORNING, RIGHT?!

24. WALKIES 2.0

Things change.

Flynn says that everything in life gets "disrupted". I call it shredding & replacing. I guess it means the same thing.

Changing human routines, though, can be quite a challenge.

Sometimes, when things change too quickly and without detailed step-by-step instruction, humans tend to get everything wrong.

It happened with our walkies.

Let me show you.

Here is the comparison between the wrong and the correct way to do it:

Because it is tough for humans to get it right,

my comrades and I are currently working on all kinds of shredding & replacing instructions. And we came up with some pretty good ones, too.

Take the solution below, for example:
- 100% green energy!
- 100% self driving.
- Total collision control.
- And it talks to you, too.
  (Non-stop!)

Coolest, right?

Flynn says that we'd be happy to pass our secrets on to the Tesla-car human. After all, we need to join forces to save our amazing Earth-ball, right?

25. DOGGIE SUPER-STARE

Doggies and cats have several amazing super-stares to choose from.

There are two basic cat stares that I have observed on Baghaval.
One is the stare that goes right through you as if you were not present (or as if you were not WORTHY of being present). The other one seems to say, "Shall I eat you now or later?".

I find both cat stares quite intimidating, to be honest with you.

Doggie stares are different, though.

One of the most common doggie stares is the *I–love–you–so–very–much–and–if–you–love–me–even–a–little–bit–back–then–you–would–not–mind–letting–me–have–that–insignificant–piece–of–food* stare.

Yeah, long name.

This stare works really well on my Tony-human while my Lassal-human is easier convinced with brainy arguments.

In her case the *I—love—you—and—you—know—that—I—love—you—and—I—know—that—you—know—that—I—love—you—and—because—love—is—totally—important—we—both—know—that—you—will—end—up—giving—me—this—tiny—piece—of—yummy—food—anyway—because—it—is—NOTHING—compared—to—my—love—for—you—so—why—wait—any—longer?* stare is the better choice.

Yeah, precise names are important. How else would you keep the stares apart?

Just to be clear, super-stares have nothing to do with common staring contests.

While super-stares are a loving & nurturing tool-thingy to train your humans, staring

contests are more about who's getting the
first big bite of the sausage.

Staring contests work well long distance (like
across a room) but they can also totally work
nose-to-nose, if necessary.

I'm rather good at staring contests. I've never
lost a staring contest but once. And that was
only because Flynn got me distracted.

There is a very special mixed form of stare:
our X-ray super-stare!

This one goes through chairs, books, windows, newspapers, and suchlike. Its main aim to is to gain your human's attention. It requires the mostest intensity from all the stares that I have mentioned above.

Don't worry, a strong will and perseverance will get you there.

DEALING WITH COMPLICATIONS.
REGISTERING EVASION MEASURES. **X-RAY ADD-ON ACTIVATED!**
OK. YOU WON. WHAT DO YOU WANT **NOW?**

And besides, the rewards are totally worth it!

***

26. TRAVELS

I love my home. And that includes the returning-home thingy.

Unfortunately, you can only return home if you go away first. So I guess I am okay with traveling to places as long as we are talking about beaches, forests, lakes, and mountains. And provided that we travel by car.

Cars are great.

The bigger ones have this comforting, deep rumbling sound that I like. Therefore, the bigger the car, the better!

My job then is to take care of the big car whenever my humans are filling it up with whatever such a car eats.

And, like everything I do, I take this job extremely seriously.

Yes, indeed, I love to travel and to go places! And I am totally well travel-equipped.

I have my own little travel-suitcase which doubles down as my travel bed. It will carry whatever my humans think I'll need and whatever I think they'll need. Hence, it will contain the usual stuff (blanket, bowl, food, ball, chewing-bone) and — unbeknownst to my humans — a few extras (replacement sticks, additional extra dirty socks, and just-in-case breakfast leftovers).

Flynn usually travels in the suitcase along with whatever book he is currently enjoying the most.

He does not care for leaving the house but he is okay with traveling as long as he has packed enough to read.

Therefore, the rest of my suitcase is always full of Flynn's books. A lot of his favorite cowboy romance novels include travel scenes and so he pretends he is on the road with them.

Still, the mostest important thing to consider

when traveling with my humans is to make sure they cannot ever leave the house without me.

I'm not saying that they might try to sneak away and leave me behind, alone. I'm just saying that they could get confused and forget to take me by accident.

This is a very sensible worry given that my humans are a bit scatterbrained.

So, when I notice that one of them is packing a suitcase, I move my napping place to the front door.

Better safe than sorry, right?

*MAKING SURE NO ONE
LEAVES THE HOUSE WITHOUT ME.*

Sometimes, though, it gets tricky when my
Tony-human is packing his special suitcase.

There is something odd about this suitcase
(apart from its shape) that makes him become
even more scatterbrained than usual.

141

I found that this special case requires rather drastic measures from my side.

＊ ＊ ＊

27. GUIDANCE AND MENTORING

Before we get to the juicy part of this chapter, we need to talk about the very first step to make our humans guidance-ready.

With this I mean: before you can begin to even think about safely training your humans, you need to first catch and secure their full attention!

That usually requires a clever bait (I use my ball) and an unusual amount of patience.

Next step would be to put your humans on the leash.

Don't feel bad about it. A leash is a very useful tool for training sessions.

Without a leash your humans will lose their focus in no time.

They will wander all over the place, take out their phone-thingies, and once that happens you won't get them to concentrate on the training anytime soon.

Once you have them on the leash, and you see your human losing focus, just give the leash a quick and hard pull into an unexpected direction. Surprise them! That usually helps to snap the focus back on you.

Be gentle but stay firm.
If you do this half-heartedly it won't work.

And always remember: It is in their very own bestest interest that you are taking charge here.

Another point is that you must respond really quickly to whatever they do. This is the only way they'll know that their actions and your reactions are connected.
This is so totally important!!!

Otherwise you'll only confuse them. And

145

confused humans are hard to guide and care for.

I had to learn this early in my little life. My humans are frightfully helpless without my constant guidance and direction. But I love them so much that I don't mind the extra work.

LITTLE HUNTERMAN'S
LIFE COACHING

ZZzzzZZzzz...

ZZZZZZ...

BECAUSE OFTEN, ALL YOU NEED
IS A SMALL CHANGE OF PERSPECTIVE.

Then again, doggies are a natural at this. It's just what we're good at, right?

146

28. THREE THINGS THE EARTH-BALL COULD USE MORE OF

There are many things on this Earth-ball in dire need of improvement.

Some of these things are tricky to grasp and control, like love.

And some of them are very complicated and difficult and need a lot of human help, like saving the big waters and the big skies and the big forests... Big things. Hairy stuff.

But there are also small things. Things that are neither difficult nor complicated.

Here are three easy things the world could use more of:

1. FAIR CROISSANT TRADE
Fair trade is totally important for a fair croissant distribution. And a fair croissant

distribution is totally important to me
EVERYONE!

2. Doggie diplomacy

When pressed to choose between two equally
good big wee-trees, you can always go for the
tiny third one, instead.

3. PILES AND MORE PILES OF FANTASTICALLY SOFT PILLOWS.

You can never have enough pillows when dealing with life's bumps and hard floorboards, right?

And whenever we've finished doing the small bits, we should be all warmed up and ready to tackle the really big and hairy stuff.

29. TV THINGIES, THE NEWS, AND A LOT OF BLACK SPAGHETTI

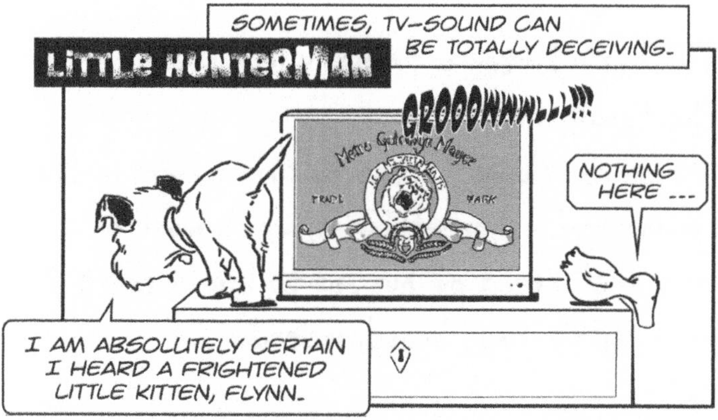

LITTLE HUNTERMAN
SOMETIMES, TV-SOUND CAN BE TOTALLY DECEIVING.
GROOOWWWLLL!!!
NOTHING HERE ...
I AM ABSOLUTELY CERTAIN I HEARD A FRIGHTENED LITTLE KITTEN, FLYNN.

I never found that kitten — even though I kept hearing it over and over. What I found, instead, were huge amounts of black spaghetti.

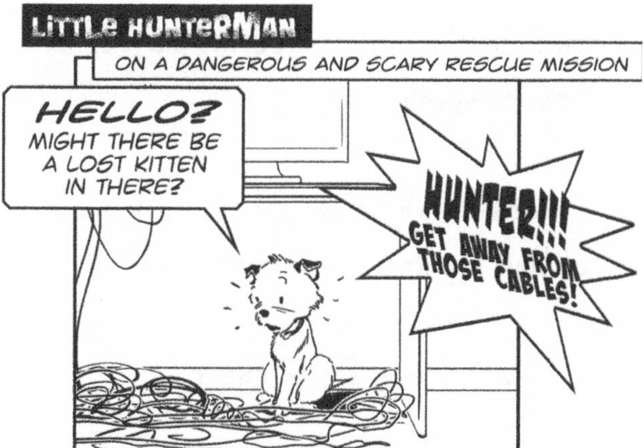

LITTLE HUNTERMAN
ON A DANGEROUS AND SCARY RESCUE MISSION
HELLO? MIGHT THERE BE A LOST KITTEN IN THERE?
HUNTER!!! GET AWAY FROM THOSE CABLES!

That black spaghetti seems to grow like weeds behind my humans' desks. It's quite worrisome! (And my humans totally hate it when I go there.)

The little kitten is probably lost somewhere in the tangle. Poor thing.
Maybe it belongs to the talking humans in the computer-tv-phone-thingies, which must be a very small breed of humans to live in there. A very, VERY small breed, indeed.

Tiny humans.
And flat, too.

A tiny, flat breed of humans in a tiny and totally flat computer-tv-phone-thingy world. With some tiny and flat kittens, maybe, to keep them company.

That's probably why many of these humans keep getting big and important stuff all wrong.
Big stuff just won't fit in there.

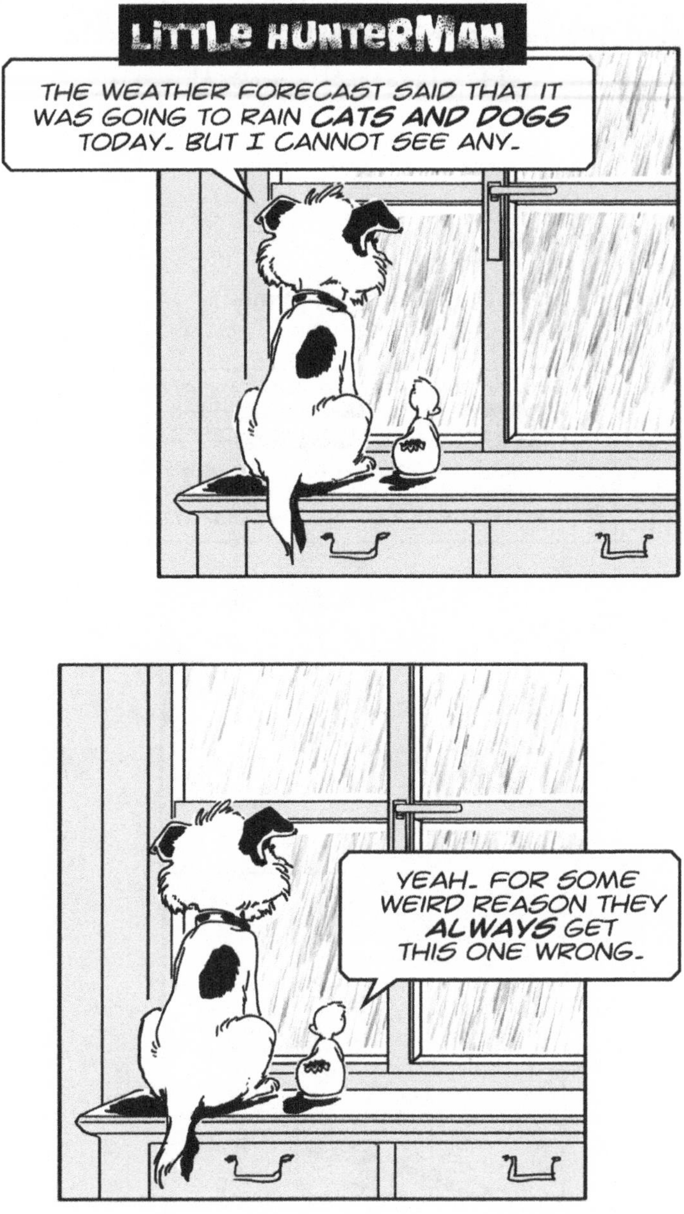
LITTLE HUNTERMAN
THE WEATHER FORECAST SAID THAT IT WAS GOING TO RAIN **CATS AND DOGS** TODAY. BUT I CANNOT SEE ANY.
YEAH. FOR SOME WEIRD REASON THEY **ALWAYS** GET THIS ONE WRONG.

And yeah, my humans insist that I leave the black spaghetti alone and play with my toys, instead.

I try. Really!
But my toys are so very boring.

It is definitely much more interesting to look for kittens and itsy bitsy humans in the black-spaghetti weeds.

I wonder why my humans can't see the obvious.

30. THE ART OF THE SQUEEZE

Picking the correct squeeze for every situation is complicated.

It obviously totally depends on WHY you are squeezing in. And WHERE it's happening.

Sometimes, you just want to feel closer to someone, or less left out, or more loved, or soothed after a nightmare, or warmer in a cold winter night.

There are other reasons, obviously. Many more reasons. Thankfully, you can mix and match all of them.

Beginners can follow my super simple PIPE strategy which is all about the planning and expert execution of one basic squeezing-in approach.

THE *PIPE* STRATEGY #01

LiTTLe HUNTeRMAN *SQUEEZING—IN LESSON FOR BEGINNERS*

PLAN

INSERT

PLACE

EXPAND

Practice the moves in slow motion. Once you have the basics down, you can add other stuff, increase the speed, try variations, and add more elements of surprise.

Remember, every squeeze-situation is different.

You will always have to adapt.
Then again, that's the fun part, right?

You'll quickly notice how squeezing in correctly will make your human super thankful and give you a lot of added benefits.

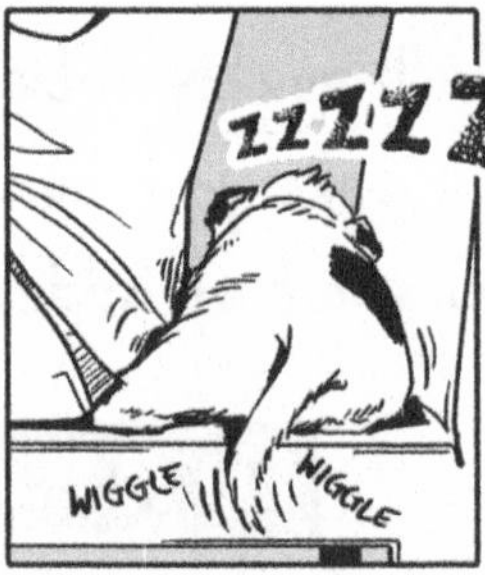
ZZZZZ
WIGGLE
WIGGLE

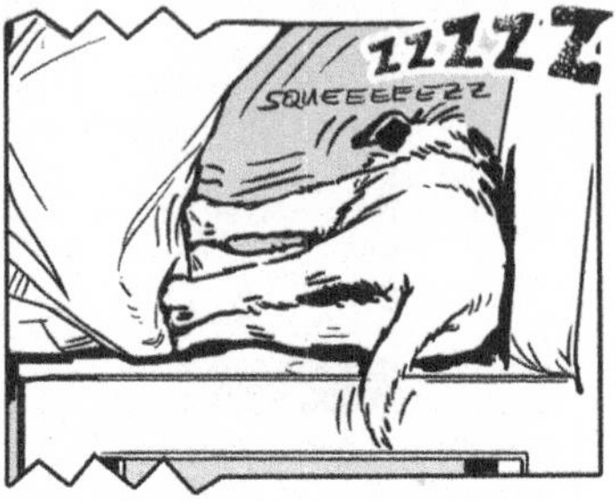
ZZZZZ
SQUEEEEEEZZ

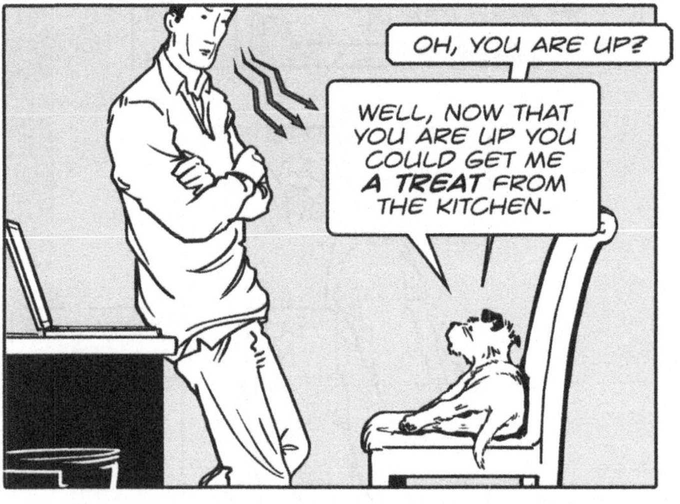
OH, YOU ARE UP?
WELL, NOW THAT YOU ARE UP YOU COULD GET ME **A TREAT** FROM THE KITCHEN.

Win-win, right?

31. PICTURES AND PHOTOBOMBS

My Lassal-human loves to take pictures.
　　Always.
　　　　Everywhere.
　　　　　　Mercilessly.

This can cause difficulties to a doggie with a busy schedule.

LiTTLe HUNTeRMaN

SOMETIMES MY LASSAL—HUMAN
AND I HAVE ONE OF OUR FUN
PHOTO—SESSIONS

It can be reeeeeeaaaaaally tricky to take care of my duties while staring into a camera.

But I try my very bestest to keep the interruptions as short as possible.

Like I said, she never seems to get enough pictures...

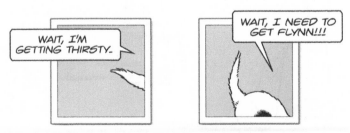

And sometimes work has to come first.

Strangely enough, though, despite the huge amount of photographs and all the posing hassle that I have to go through, she mostly ends up drawing me anyway.

Weird, right?

I, on the other paw side, have my very own way of getting fantastical pictures taken.

And of all the things that I've tested so far, photobombing is totally the mostest fun!

The picture below is one of my favorites.

It looks a bit messy because I dragged it outside to show it to my friend Hinkemann Crow and it got a tiny bit wet along the way.

LE HUNTERMAN

I sooo totally love my family!!!

32. MY HUMANS AND I AGREE ON (ALMOST) EVERYTHING

Some doggies say that you should never ever let your humans onto the couch with you. They will also insist that you need to be through the door first to make sure that your home is safe and that there's no intruder in the house.

Other doggies don't care too much about these things but insist, instead, that your humans should most definitely only ever eat after they have fed you first.

Most agree, though, that you definitely need to make sure that we all take care of each other and spread the love to avoid worries and tummy aches.

Then again, everyone seems to have an opinion on everything. Humans are no exception.

At home, though, there is no real conflict.

LITTLE HUNTERMAN
RRRIINNG RRRIINNG
HI MOM, HOW LOVELY TO HEAR FROM YOU ...
... YOU HAVE BEEN READING THE CARTOON? OH, THAT'S NICE! ...
... YOU DO **NOT** APPROVE OF DOGS SLEEPING IN OUR BEDS? I SEE ... TERRIBLE HYGIENE? YES. MOST CERTAINLY!
NO NEED TO WORRY, MOM. **IT IS JUST A CARTOON!** WE MAKE THAT STUFF UP... EXACTLY! ... IT IS NOT REAL LIFE! IN REAL LIFE HUNTERMAN TOTALLY KNOWS HIS PLACE ...

My humans and I always agree on the mostest important stuff.

With us, it's never about who's the boss. Instead, it's all about who loves whom mostest.

And about who shows love the bestest.

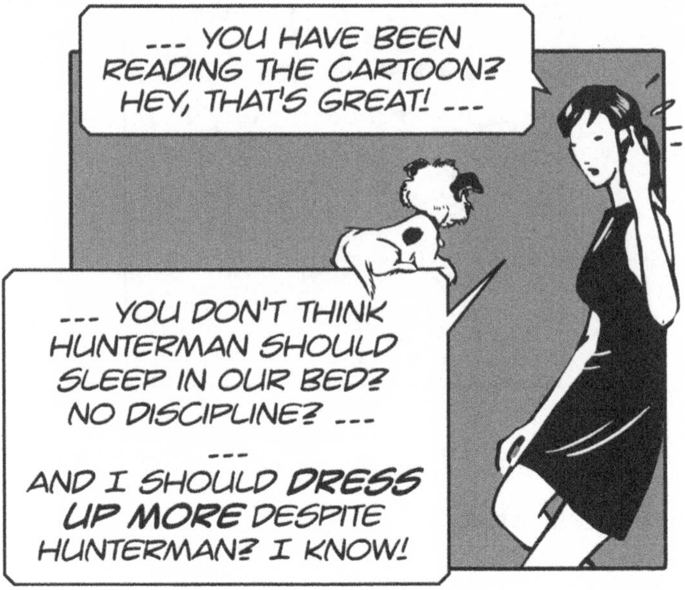
--- YOU HAVE BEEN READING THE CARTOON? HEY, THAT'S GREAT! ---
--- YOU DON'T THINK HUNTERMAN SHOULD SLEEP IN OUR BED? NO DISCIPLINE? ---
--- AND I SHOULD **DRESS UP MORE** DESPITE HUNTERMAN? I KNOW!

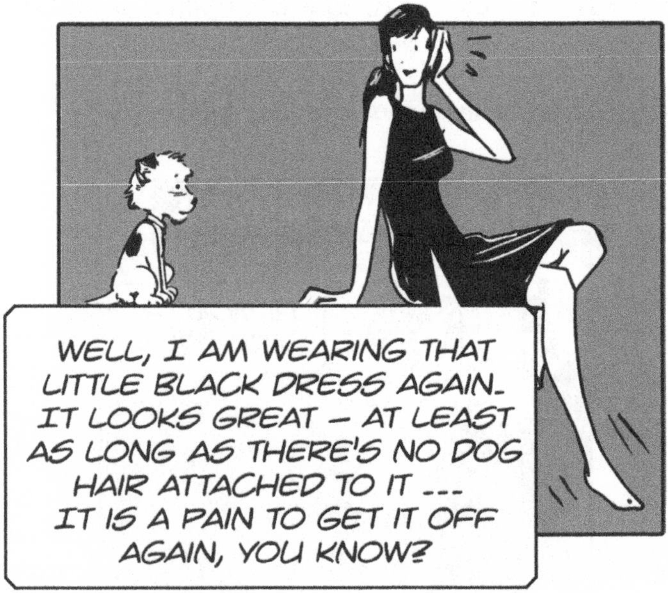
WELL, I AM WEARING THAT LITTLE BLACK DRESS AGAIN. IT LOOKS GREAT – AT LEAST AS LONG AS THERE'S NO DOG HAIR ATTACHED TO IT --- IT IS A PAIN TO GET IT OFF AGAIN, YOU KNOW?

You need rules, of course. Rules are important to make humans feel safe, and in control, and at peace. But in my home, all rules and priorities are crystal clear, totally logical, and shared by all of us.

And that's totally all that counts.

33. THE END

It always happens. We always seem to get to the end around here.

Oops, false alarm.

THE REAL END
The Story's Little Tail

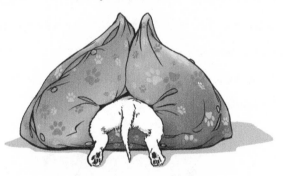

Okay, I admit, that is MY tail.
But it is kinda my story as well,
so I hope it's fine.

SHORT AFTERBARK

Now that my cartoon self has his own book, I keep worrying about my for-real doggie-self. Shouldn't my real self be doing something as cool or even cooler than my illustrated self?

A FANTASTICAL JOB, maybe?

There was a time when I was a highly sought after SOUND ENGINEER for my Tony-human and his music thingies. It fizzled out, though, when I voluntarily started to fill in as a background singer; although that is probably a coincidence.

A cool job that requires little work from my part is the secret agent stuff. I've spent hours and hours as an active UNDER COVER DOUBLE AGENT.

("Double" because of Flynn, of course.)

That was kinda fun and I hardly ever fell asleep for real.

(Obviously, there are always ways to improve your under cover skills. It's a lifelong learning thingy.)

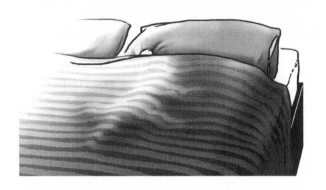

A much more active job is the one of a SEMI-PROFESSIONAL BED-BALL PLAYER.

Unfortunately, these fun times always end rather abruptly when my humans stop throwing the ball.

So, maybe that's no good. It leaves me too little control.

Once, I played with the thought of becoming my very own CROISSANT BAKERY OWNER. I even started dressing the part.

As a good bakery owner, I'd have to make sure that my customers get the yummiest croissants ever. Which obviously means that I'd have to test each croissants first — just an itsy bitsy tiny bite...

But every time I practice this step I get a weird flash combined with an unexplainable lapse of memory.
And when my memory returns, there is never any croissant left! Someone must be stealing them while I am out of memory!!!!!!!!!!

Super weirdly strange, right?

So, the croissant-backery-owner option is on hold until I solve the mystery of the disappearing croissants and catch the thief.

Anyway...

Another task I really enjoy is to spend hours and hours as a COLD-WATER CHANNEL-SWIMMER doggie.

I could do this forever, but it triggers an urge in my humans to try out their newest blanket wrapping methods on me, which totally interrupts my flow.

I've also repeatedly acted as the LOCAL
DUCK SWIM TRAINER. It's only a seasonal
job, though, which is sad. Before you know it,
they grow up and think they can swim out into
the mighty river alone. Then you keep having
to rescue them.

179

Ducks are a bit of work. Then again, I have my little Flynn. I don't mind a bit of work.

Another idea I am toying with is to become an OFFICIAL CROW WHISPERER!

I bet that my friend Hinkemann Crow would give me a head-start in this job. He is a totally patient and kind crow who often joins me on my nighttime walkies. He taught me everything I know about crows — although I'm still having troubles with their language. Crow is a tough language to bark. Then again, according to the job description it would be all about WHISPERING, right? If I'd whisper really softly no one could possibly hear my doggie-accent. Maybe I could up that a notch and just THINK ALOUD?! ☺

There is one issue, though: While I totally LOVE my friend Hinkemann, I quite dislike the crows that once mobbed and hurt him. I would only enjoy this job if I could choose which crow to whisper with.

What I ALWAYS enjoy, though, are naps! I could become a PROFESSIONAL NAPPER AND CUSHION TESTER. That would be the mostest natural thing for me to do and completely easiest. I could do it in my sleep!

But wouldn't that be a very selfish job choice?
Especially considering that the Earth-ball
totally needs A PROPER COUCH DESIGNER
to account for some reasonable couch-sticks!

I could also think reeeeeally long term and become A FANTASTICALLY SCARY GHOST. Not a bad option, all thingies considered.

Then again, while I've not gotten much of a practice as a ghost, yet, I am an enormously EXPERIENCED OVEN-GUARD...

... who'll totally go the extra round to retrieve each and every cookie — no matter where it falls.

Another job I definitely always enjoy is the one of the COURAGEOUS MUD-HOLE CONQUISTADOR...

... if it were not for the scary bathtub-aftermaths.

Then, there is this one job that I am already famous for: In case you did not know, I'm the merciless Hunterman SUPER-SHREDDER!!!

I specialize in delivery boxes. And in extra small shreds.

But I'm happy to expand to birthday and Christmas presents of any kind. Or moving boxes. Anything that needs speedy and professional unwrapping is totally my thing.

Soooooo many fantastical job-opportunities, right? Too many, really.

I cannot decide. I like everything! How can you possibly choose one thing when you want to keep doing all of it?

How to decide these totally important things?

* * *

Maybe I'll just try to be YOUR BESTEST FRIEND, instead,...

After all, with so many amazing friends and totally cool comrades, I hope it's fine if I just stay being plain little old worried me.

I like this choice the mostest.

* * *

Download this book's first-ever written chapter. (Which my human THREW AWAY!!!)

I had to totally dig around for it — which is why it looks a bit messy.
www.littlehunterman.com/
buried-chapter

BE MY FRIEND, FOLLOW ALONG & GET MY MONDAY CARTOON WEE-WEES

These wees MIGHT end up in the next book...
(Coolest, right?.)

Join us here:

www.littlehunterman.com/monday-cartoon

OTHER LITTLE HUNTERMAN BOOKS & STUFF

www.LittleHunterman.com/stuff

Throughout the years, I've learned a lot about humans and rubber ducks. And I'm writing it all down to save you the trouble of having to find it out for yourself.
That's the EASY part.

The HARD part is to wait for my human's illustrations. Not that we need illustrations, but it makes my human happy to feel useful.

I ONLY WISH SHE'D HURRY A BIT MORE! You'd TOTALLY help me drag her along by leaving us an honest

 **REVIEW-THINGY**
(Pretty please? ☺)

ABOUT HUNTER LASSAL

My Lassal-human has recently morphed from a storyboard artist into a scribbling biographer of a sweet, ~~wimpy~~ fearless, and utterly ~~worried~~ BIG ~~little~~ Parson Russell Terrier, Hunterman (Yay, that's me!), and his nerdy rubber duck, Flynn.

Together we write as HUNTER LASSAL to share the mostest fantastical stories and important doggie insights with my animal comrades and human friends.
We'd be totally thrilled if you'd join our little family.

Bring your human too, if you like...
... and maybe a croissant, or two?!

CAN YOU SEE HOW LITTLE I STILL AM? *ANOTHER CROISSANT* WOULD TOTALLY FOR SURE HELP ME GROW!

Your BIG friend
Little Hunterman

WHO'S WHO ANYWAY?

<u>LITTLE HUNTERMAN</u>

Little Hunterman is the cartoon dog version of a rather shy and risk-averse Parson Russell Terrier called Hunter.

He fears open windows but loves to be outside, dislikes dog food but treasures found leftovers (and croissants), detests changes in his holy routines and rituals but delights in extra rounds if they include rat-chases of any kind.

Little Hunterman has a strong sense of order and how the world around him is supposed to behave. No exceptions — unless he came up with the new rule himself.

FLYNN (ADMIRAL FLYNN VAN KWIITSCH)

Flynn, a rubber duck, had his tail chewed off by a young and rather overexcited Hunterman a few years back. Since then, for fear of sinking, Flynn has been terrified of anything resembling water, avoiding any contact with it — a fact that makes personal hygiene rather challenging.

Hunterman has accepted the responsibility for his actions and not only became Flynn's best friend and protector but also carries the little rubber duck around with him whenever he goes out. Because of his smelly self, Flynn's place is on Hunterman's tail, and thus as far away from the sensitive dog nose as possible.

Flynn can be an arrogant and self absorbed little rascal, but we all love him dearly.

<u>LASSAL-HUMAN</u>

Lassal-human is an engineer turned artist.

Several years ago, while attempting to take more breaks from sitting and working non-stop at her desk, she got to know a little Parson Russell Terrier and fell madly in love with him.

Back then, she used to work for big international commercial agencies and corporations. Now, she works pretty much only for Little Hunterman.

With a Little Hunterman in tow, her life has gotten so much more complicated, but ah, so extraordinarily more rewarding!

TONY-HUMAN

Tony-human is an architect and Lassal-human's partner in crime. Together, they share the worries and joys that come with having a Little Hunterman.

While Lassal-human is the stern one who insists on being the leash-leader, Tony-human calmly and without fail allows Hunterman to wrap him around his little paws — and to pull him along.

Hunterman loves him dearly for this.

(And he also loves him for the zombie-chases and extra croissants.)

Made in the USA
Coppell, TX
06 December 2020

43446408R00132